Portland in old picture postcards

by
Stuart Morris

Second edition

European Library - Zaltbommel/Netherlands MCMLXXXIV

GB ISBN 90 288 2647 5

European Library in Zaltbommel/Netherlands publishes among other things the following series:

IN OLD PICTURE POSTCARDS *is a series of books which sets out to show what a particular place looked like and what life was like in Victorian and Edwardian times. A book about virtually every town in the United Kingdom is to be published in this series. By the end of this year about 175 different volumes will have appeared. 1,250 books have already been published devoted to the Netherlands with the title* **In oude ansichten.** *In Germany, Austria and Switzerland 500, 60 and 15 books have been published as* **In alten Ansichten;** *in France by the name* **En cartes postales anciennes** *and in Belgium as* **En cartes postales anciennes** *and/or* **In oude prentkaarten** *150 respectively 400 volumes have been published.*

For further particulars about published or forthcoming books, apply to your bookseller or direct to the publisher.

This edition has been printed and bound by Grafisch Bedrijf De Steigerpoort in Zaltbommel/Netherlands.

INTRODUCTION

Few places have been transformed so dramatically by man as the Island of Portland. The pictures in this book cover a period of phenominal change of the Portland scene. The earliest ones were taken at a time when the Tophill plateau of the Island consisted of modest villages, still widely separated by fields laid out in classic Mediaeval strip pattern, while on the steep escarpments of Underhill dense housebuilding was already filling the gaps and gardens between the settlements of Chiswell and Fortuneswell.

During those fifty years the annual extraction of up to 100,000 tons of the famed Portland Stone was to devour much of Tophill's rural landscape. New efficient stone masonry works were established and became major employers. While quarrying on a vast scale had continued on and off since the times of Inigo Jones and Sir Christopher Wren in the seventeenth century, it was only late Victorian mechanisation which enabled workings to take huge bites at random into the open fields. This move away from the traditional cliff-edge sites, where even years of quarrying had made little impact on the natural coastal character, caused more than the loss of a historic landscape.

The earlier photographs included here show the last of the Island's commercial sheep flock, which, deprived of its grazing land, disappeared from Portland completely by 1930.

Beyond the conversion of a pastoral landscape into a network of quarries, the fifty year timespan we are looking at saw the impact of the great Royal Naval Base developments; the literal remoulding of Verne Hill, Portland's 490 feet (149 metres) high summit, into a fortress – a monument of Victorian grandeur. We cover the period of transformation brought by a piped water supply and main drainage schemes, a public gas supply, asphalted roads, new parks, a railway to the centre of the Island at Easton, not to mention motor transport and the first of many land-hungry housing estates.

During that half-century parts of the Island changed beyond recognition. How more remarkable is it then that so much of the original character of the place and its people did survive.

The casual visitor is always amazed that this rugged apparently barren island can hold such a spellbinding interest to so many.

For an island only 4½ miles long by 1½ miles at its widest, Portland has supremely rich character. This is well illustrated by the range of subjects covered by this selection of postcard photographs. What the pictures cannot show is the folklore, the old Portland characters – their stories told in colourful island tones –, that with settings like Church Ope and Chesil Coves, and the intimate old quarry cuttings, have inspired more artists and poets than most conventionally 'attractive' places.

Many of the photographs were taken around the turn of the century, when the resident population was around nine thousand, but adding to this number were several thousands of military, naval and prison personnel. The earliest Portlanders of whom we know lived near The Bill in Mesolithic times seven thousand years ago. Stone circles and megaliths at The Grove

on the east coast and elsewhere on the Island point to ancient pagan worship, and there has been abundant evidence of Iron Age and Roman occupation, notably at Verne Hill, at Fortuneswell and at Southwell.
Between 1850 and 1930 thousands of artefacts from ancient times were discovered as quarries were opened in the fields of Tophill. Today we can only guess at the significance of many of these, for the sites were totally destroyed. Thankfully 1932 saw the conversion of an old cottage at Wakeham into a fine museum. This provided a treasure-house for collections of at least some items from all periods which would otherwise have been scattered or lost.
Portland was a Royal Manor in Saxon times, and still is so today. The influence of the Crown on the Island's development over the last nine hundred years is reflected in its landscape and throughout its history. Naturally as Lord of the Manor the Crown was a major land holder, owning most of the open spaces including Chesil Beach and the demesne farm near Easton. The ancient Court Leet still has real authority, although this was reduced by changes in the land laws in 1925. Around the cliffs and in wide swathes between the Portland villages are the common lands, where the residents for time out of mind have had valuable rights, including the right to graze sheep and cattle, to dig stone and to fish. The Court Leet's duty was – and is – to protect these rights. Even the Crown by law must respect these islanders' privileges.
Whilst farming, the stone industry and the Court Leet have been the major factors in Island development over the centuries, the predominance of the sea has shaped the pattern of life here. Chiswell has long suffered from its destructive force, but that village also owes its existence to local fishing which always provided its living, until the time of change covered by this book. Smuggling and countless shipwrecks brought their counterparts, the coastguards and customs services, and the lighthouses. The natural anchorage of Portland Roads was developed into one of the world's largest man-made harbours. We are fortunate that the last stages of this great work were recorded by the early photographers. The building and defence of the harbour led to the establishment of the prison and major Admiralty departments.
This unique peninsula of limestone is linked to the mainland only by Chesil Beach, the world-famous feature that means so much to Portland. This 16 mile (26 kilometres) long bank of shingle provides no firm ground for road or path, so until a bridge was built across Smallmouth Passage in 1839, Portland was in all but the purest sense an island. This insularity preserved customs, folklore and a character quite distinct from other parts of Dorset, much of which survived the overwhelming changes of the late nineteenth and early twentieth centuries. These photographs span that era of transition.
I would like to acknowledge the help given by many Portland friends over many years, without whose generosity the collection could not have been built up.

1. There is no better position from which to view the world-famous Chesil Beach than from Priory, on the top of Portland. Photographers have stood on this spot since the pioneer days of the camera, to record a scene which is constantly changing. Light through a moist sea atmosphere produces an infinite variety of colours and hues, and some of the most spectacular sunsets to be seen from the south coast of England. Seen here in 1892, the fields of Lancridge and Long Close gave dairy and garden produce for the people of Maiden Well, Chiswell and Fortuneswell. Beyond the houses can be seen the Mere, a tidal inlet that harboured small boats since pre-Roman times. The great shingle bank, vanishing north-westwards towards Abbotsbury, is pinched between the waters of West Bay on the left, and Portland Harbour.

2. In this view some thirty-five years later, the old Mere is being drained of its waters for land reclamation by the Admiralty. The first of the great cylindrical storage tanks to store fuel for the new ships of the Royal Navy were built in 1906. By 1930, rows of these monsters had encroached upon the isthmus, but so striking are the natural land-forms that even these do little to mar the vista. Beyond the harbour are the fields of Wyke Regis and Belfield, most of which were built over in the 1950's. The Dorset Ridgeway forms the skyline. The hand-crane in the foreground was the second of two on the site at Priory used for transferring quarried stone blocks on to the Portland (or Merchants) Railway. A 'Sentinal' steam waggon can be seen here preparing to return to the quarries for its next load.

3. The houses of Fortuneswell spill out at random from the steep-sided Tilleycoombe, nestling below the slopes of Verne Hill. The large building, upper centre in this 1895 view, is the old St. John's School, built in 1857, and the rows of cottages descending to the left, were part of the ancient separate hamlet of Mallams. The precipitous track in the foreground is Old Hill, until the early nineteenth century the main link between Underhill and Tophill. A robust handrail set in stone pillars helped walkers, but only the strongest of horses could pull a load up to the top of the island by this route. Severe damage was inflicted on Fortuneswell during the last war, from bombs intended for the nearby Naval Base. Among the casualties were many of the properties on the right and the old St. John's School. Fortunately the children were home at the time.

4. A Hovis bread ban trundles up Meissner's Knapp towards Fortuneswell in the 1920's. The three storey buildings on the left housed a bank, a bakery and a photographer's studio. Beyond these the pointed gable of Fortuneswell Primitive Methodist Church can be seen. This was built in 1869 for one of the three factions of that Church that were well established on the island. The Church closed in 1970, but the building has now been lovingly converted into a 'live' theatre by Portland's drama club. This view of the castellated tower of St. John's Church of 1839 (centre) was completely obliterated some twelve years after this picture was taken, by the Regal Cinema, – a stark building which fell far short of the great 'Art Deco' cinema architecture of that era. The tallest building on the right was the Royal Hotel, converted into flats in the 1950's, and Prospect Place was so named for its distant view of West Bay.

5. This is the original heart of Fortuneswell. The remains of the old well stones can still be seen near the little girl in white. The fine and never-failing spring that fed this well had been known at least since Roman times. A legend refers to a temple to the 'Goddess of Fortune' nearby which may have given its name to the well. Here in about 1908 this bustling road was lined with dozens of little shops, and echoed to the sounds of street traders, horse carts and traction engines. The three storey buildings are of the mid-Victorian age, their loftiness making the narrow street – already shielded by the high land on two sides – quite dark except on the brightest days. The bay windowed buildings beyond the old Sun Inn were pulled down after heavy wartime bomb damage. The spring water was piped away out of sight after Portland's mains water supply was laid on in 1901. Although unseen, its fresh spring-water still flows down to Chiswell and the sea.

6. At the commercial hub of Fortuneswell is the General Post Office (centre), built around 1860. Until that period the Underhill area's economy was based upon fishing, sheep farming and a little general trading. Transformation came in the wake of the monumental government works of the Harbour Breakwater and the Coastal Defences. This street was within easy walking distance for the engineers, administrators and skilled workers employed on those projects. The new found economy built several banks, many public houses and hotels, drapery and grocery emporiums and countless small shops. The stone-mason's art was exploited to the full in these elaborately carved Victorian facades, right up to the eaves, where the detail was lost to the busy passer-by. The elegant gas-lit pendants projecting from the provisions shop in this 1898 photograph would have given a romantic glow to the night-time street scene.

7. Young girls in their pristine-white frills seem to dominate this Wesleyan Sunday School procession along Fortuneswell's narrow road. A scene from a more sedate age, before twentieth century traffic almost strangled the commercial life out of this main street. Processions of every description were very popular between about 1870 and 1930, and the children needed little persuasion to take part. Until the mid-nineteenth century, for many Portland children particularly the girls, the Sunday School was the only sort of formal education they ever had.

8. Although this postcard was sent in 1904, the photograph was taken a few years earlier. This terrace on the west side of Fortuneswell had as good a selection of buildings from different periods as one could find in one block. Note the eighteenth century house on the left. Unlike the modest cottage next door which was faced in uncoursed rubble, this building was of the best coursed Portland Stone ashlar, and an early etching shows that it originally had a classical portico doorway. This house was bought by Robert Brackenbury, a Methodist pioneer who came to Portland in 1791 to sort out the 'den of vice and iniquity of every description' as the island was described to him. The name of this little corner of Underhill is 'Bedlam'. The whole row was demolished after the war, the last to go being Brackenbury's very sound house. The site is now a car park.

9. This is the chapel in Fortuneswell, that the wealthy Robert Carr Brackenbury built as a gift to Portlanders in 1792. A finely proportioned Georgian building, it had a simple classical facade, and a small bell turret. By 1837, it regularly had congregations of six hundred or more, – good going from an Underhill population of less than two thousand. In its large grounds a little day school was opened on 15th May 1845, in an unpretentious stone building which in 1982 was still serving that purpose as part of a larger school still bearing Brackenbury's name. A small graveyard was established alongside this Chapel, and among those buried there were the bodies of a Missionary and his wife, only newly married, who died with fifteen others in a schooner wrecked on nearby Chesil Beach in November 1838.

10. A fine new Chapel was erected in Fortuneswell by local builder John Patten in 1899. (He is seen standing before the old Chapel gateway in photograph 9.) Such was the demand for seating that the congregation had outgrown Brackenbury's original Church by the 1890's. The Trustees launched an architectural competition for the design. The winner was chosen and memorial stones were laid on 30th May 1898, amid great ceremony. Soon the pseudo-Gothic spendour of its facade was to exude the confidence and pride that abounded in Queen Victoria's last years. Four years after its opening in 1900, a grand organ was installed at considerable cost. This must have had an awe-inspriring sound at a time when for most Portlanders musical experience was limited to the pedal harmonium, piano or musical box.

11. Edward VII, King of Great Britain, Emperor of India, passing through Fortuneswell in 1902 with the minimum of fuss, and remarkably few onlookers. Not that Portlanders did not have a special regard for the Monarchy, but informal royal visits to the various Government establishments here were fairly frequent. Being a Royal Manor, the island has close and historic connections with the Crown. King George III also frequented Portland while based at his seaside lodge at Weymouth, and his favourite haunt here was the Royal Portland Arms in Fortuneswell. He was particularly fond of the landlady's special plum pudding, and he made many friends (of both sexes) in the locality.

12. The vibrant colour and sound of marching military regiments, each led through Fortuneswell by its resident band, became a regular experience for Portland folk after the completion of the great Verne Citadel in 1872. This is the 2nd Dorset Regiment, which was stationed here between 1902-1904 and again in 1919. Trees marked the upper limit of the densely developed Underhill district, beyond which can be glimpsed the backcloth of the steep escarpment called 'Royal'. The pathway up Old Hill, and the gentler New Road ascend from here to the top of the island. Comben's China shop was later converted into a bank. Next door was a hardware shop and then Underhill's Fire Station. Although still with a crushed stone surface when this picture was taken, the road itself had been drastically improved since the early nineteenth century, when a stone-lined ditch carried a tiny stream into old culverts further down the hill.

13. A procession of yet a different kind wends its way through Fortuneswell in about 1904. Here it is contingent of convicts en route for the Grove Prison. The charmingly picturesque cottages at the foot of New Road (lower left) were of Georgian origin. With characteristic stone-slat roofs, the corner building took its name, Yew Tree Cottage, from the dark object seen affixed to the front of the house. This was an enormous fossilised tree, which was found in a quarry at West Cliff, not far above this area. Next door was Antedeluvian Cottage, with its stone mullioned windows and portico entrance. A smuggler's tunnel was reputed to have started from its site. In the 1890's this was the residence of the island's Medical Officer of Health, Dr. Parsons. Both houses were built by wealthy quarry owner Thomas Gilbert in 1777. They were acquired by Portland Council and demolished in the 1920's to make way for new Council Offices.

14. By 1930, Portland's own Council had become responsible for most public services, including electricity, gas, water, highways and drainage. The site of the cottages featured in photograph 13 was chosen for these purpose-built offices. Faced, of course, with finest Portland stone, but on a steel frame, lavish use was made of solid oak, teak and stainless steel, for which the best craftsmen of builders, Jesty and Baker of Castletown, were employed. The Offices were opened in September 1934, and for a while electric floodlights illuminated the fresh white facade – the more impressive as Portland had only had mains electricity for two years. This was exactly half way through the life of the old Portland Council, for in 1974, a new Borough incorporating neighbouring Weymouth was formed.

15. Chiswell is one of Portland's oldest settlements founded literally on a bed of shingle at one of the few easily accessible parts of the island's coast. Fishing provided the living, and robust, solid stone cottages were the homely shelter from the prevailing south westerlies. In this picture, taken in about 1898, two and three story Georgian and earlier houses on the left, with their backs to the beach face the old village square. A gas lamp is the finial on top of a large stone cistern in the road which stored water for domestic use. This area was inhabited in Romano-British times, and the village of 'Coesl' was ravaged by the Vikings in 787 and by Pirates and plunderers in the succeeding three hundred years. The early stone hovels, some even seaward of the present beach crest, through time and the relentless encroachment of the beach, were one by one replaced by new buildings. Beneath many cottages were cellars for storage of contraband goods, for smuggling was a shaddowy feature of life on seventeenth and eighteenth century Portland.

16. This is Brandy Row, the main way to Chesil Cove. The name hints at the one-time smuggling of these parts. Tudor and Jacobean cottages rose beyond firm ground onto the shingle beach crest itself. It is clear from this 1902 photograph that the houses lining the little streets and passages to the beach had immense character. They were functional and warm, but lacking what we now call 'essential amenities'. Because of this the Portland Council before the last War condemned these and over a hundred others in the area and ordered their demolition. Sweeping aside protests of residents and eminant architects the authorities thus achieved what centuries of raging sea storms had failed to do – the systematic destruction of the heart of an ancient village. Gaping holes and half-cleared ruins still testified fifty years later to the rough justice imposed on Chiswell, whose only crime was being old. Only at the seaward fringe did the mighty power of the sea sometimes win, – the ancient ruin at the top of Brandy Row here was probably last inhabited before the catastrophic storm of 1824 when thirty-six houses were destroyed.

17. Showing signs of neglect in its final years, the original charm of this old cottage in Brandy Row still shows through. The passageway, where the baker's boy is standing, led to a small courtyard with another three or four houses behind. The locals thus called this place 'Entry'. Flat, stable land being so scarce in this part of Portland, covered passageways were used in several places to give access to odd corners of land. Many thatched cottages of similar design were built on Portland in the seventeenth century. The thatch possibly came from Weymouth's Radipole Lake with other materials from withy beds above Fortuneswell and at Southwell. Buildings of earlier and later periods used much local stone 'slatt' for roof coverings. Great timbers from shipwrecks still support roofs of many Portland cottages. This house was finally condemned and partially demolished in about 1905, although its little arched doorway may still be seen in the wall of a fishermen's store.

18. Big Ope, a short street of thick-walled fishermen's cottages, climbs the leeward slope of Chesil Beach. These 'Opes' not only gave access to the sea, they did so for the sea. Huge seas flowing over and through the massive shingle bank have had to be reckoned with here since the beginning of recorded time. Founded on nothing but silt and pebble, these houses had to withstand lashings from some of the most severe storms known on the British coast. Floodwaters regularly cascaded down the street, and often through the lower floors of the buildings. With every overtopping of the crest the beach has crept further into the village. In this 1898 photograph the street merges with the beach, the crest of which is on the skyline. Only one pair of the cottages – on the right – has survived the hand of twentieth century demolition merchants.

19. Chiswell, as with other parts of the island, was well provided with inns and public houses. By the 1850's the needs of workers and sailors from the nearby Portland Harbour had to be catered for, as well as those of fishermen. This was the Lord Clyde Inn, towards the north end of the village. Having its back to the beach, the lessons of previous builders in the area had to be heeded so floodways were built in below the floor. In this flood of 1924, the Landlord opened the ducts as usual and seawater can be seen gushing from beneath the public bar. While sea flooding has always been accepted as a fact of life, the distress and tragedy it caused were none the less for that. The Lord Clyde Inn was closed after bomb damage during the 1939-1945 War and its shell was finally cleared away in 1962.

20. For centuries, people of Chiswell have bravely suffered countless floods. Seawater has come through or over the beach on average every five years or so in south-westerly storms and sea-swells. This is the 1924 flood again, some twenty years after engineers first proposed flood prevention schemes, and thirty-five years before the major protection projects started. The cottages here at the bottom of Brandy Row withstood even the 1824 deluge, and a water-marked mirror from the first floor bedroom of one of them – now in Portland Museum – is a remarkable indicator of the height of that flood. The all dominating beach is only a few paces away from these doors. Note that the older pair of cottages, right, is set lower than the road, hinting at the original ground level of earlier times. Successive houses were built higher to lessen the flood risk. This corner of Chiswell village has survived intact, and has now been given new security for the future under the protection of a massive sea wall, built in 1958-1965.

21. Portland Fair, in early November, is the traditional time for island revelry. It is held by ancient custom and like most fairs was originally a sheep and cattle event. Until the 1860's, this fair was held at Fortuneswell, but it then moved into the streets of Chiswell, when the accent became more on fun – much to the disgust of island religious leaders who wanted the spectacle banned! Seen here in 1906 are the horsedrawn showmen's waggons, some of which had travelled hundreds of miles to be here, for the annual Portland Fair was the end of the show season. The power of steam was soon harnessed into the fairground rides and organs, providing undreampt of sensations of movement, sound and smell! Far and away, the most impressive machine regularly brought to Portland Fair was the 'Gondolas', a steam ride built in 1898, one of the most ornate ever devised, covered with cut-glass mirrors and gilt. Its last visit was in 1977, and it is now preserved in a Norfolk museum.

22. The year is 1897 and cab drivers await their next fare by the station in Victoria Square. The Royal Victoria Lodge Hotel, right, was a remarkably clean and bright design for the late nineteenth century. It was built on the site of a reputedly haunted Poor House dating from 1781. Victoria Square at this time was at its proudest. Open to Chiswell Village to the south, an elegant terrace of houses formed the beach side facing the Lodge, and on the north was the railway terminus. Cabs took train visitors to see the sights, including the convicts at work in the Admiralty Quarries. The following decades brought increasing neglect and dereliction. The closure of the railway in 1952, of the adjoining gas works and the constant threat of sea flooding, all took toll on this place. The old station was demolished in 1969 for a new road layout, but the Hotel thrives, and schemes are afoot to revitalise this gateway to Portland.

23. Little Common was a grassy but featureless foothill of the Great Verne Hill Common when the Council decided in July 1896 to commemorate Queen Victoria's Diamond Jubilee. It was to be transformed into a magnificent recreation ground, but eight years passed before 'Victoria Gardens' came to fruition. On 25th May 1904, the town band played at the grand opening before thousands of people. This picture was taken some three years later. Over £2,000 was spent on flower beds, six thousand shrubs, a croquet lawn, bowling green, rockeries and a parade. The central feature was a fine bandstand, by Messrs. Hill and Smith, and the whole area was lit by dozens of coloured gas lamps. The croquet lawn has given way to tennis courts, the bandstand was demolished in 1967, and the soft glowing lamps have long gone, but the Gardens are still enjoyed by Underhill's present generation.

24. By 1880, when this photograph was taken, Castletown had already undergone a great upheaval. Only thirty years earlier there was no more than a handful of cottages along one street, with little courts leading out of it, all sandwiched between the mighty Verne Hill and the beach of Portland Roads (anchorage). King Henry VIII's Portland Castle nearby, which had given the area its name, had solidly dominated this part of the island since 1530. Castletown Beach was the most sheltered and accessible beach on the island, a good base for generations of fishermen. In the hundred years since the photographer recorded this scene, most of the beach has been lost under naval and commercial developments, and what remains has been decimated by a haphazard clutter of huts and fencing. Between the numerous pubs, the sailors could find the Post Office, boot shop, coffee bar and a Reading Room. H.M. Customs House is on the left.

25. Construction of the Breakwaters for the creation of the harbour of refuge from 1847 had the greatest impact of all here at Castletown. A string of impressive hotels arose, their names unmistakably boasting this new influence: 'The Portland Roads', 'The Royal Breakwater', 'The Prince Albert', and 'The Sailors Return'. Only the 'Castle Hotel' and the 'Jolly Sailor', remained to represent the old order. The little lean-to against the Castle Hotel was a barber's room – a shave and haircut for a few pence. This was set much lower than the present road, its floor being at about original beach level, for this side was reclaimed from the foreshore when the stone pier was built in 1826. A Salvation Army hostel now stands by this sport.

26. In 1826, a group of local stone merchants leased a section of Castletown Beach from the Crown to build a pier. Originally built of timber, this provided a large working platform for stone to be loaded from railway trucks onto stone barges. The pier was later rebuilt in stone and proved to be a very valuable asset to the area. On the right in this picture are cranes loading stone possibly destined for London's Regent Street, or another of the capital's great building works of that era. This was a balmy summer day before World War One, and some of these ladies in their Edwardian finery, having stepped ashore from one of Cosens Paddle Steamers from Weymouth, were tempted by penny-in-slot chocolate machines at the pier gate. The visitor would then watch the Navy at work, or take a cab to other parts of the island.

27. This site is the springboard of one Victorian Britain's greatest engineering projects. From Portland Nor, on the island's north-east corner, the giant arms of the Breakwater were formed to protect the anchorage of Portland Roads. The scheme received Royal assent in 1847, and the first two arms heavily defended and fortified were declared complete by the Prince of Wales in 1872, only eighteen years before this photograph was taken. James Meadows Rendell was the first Engineer-in-Chief. His successor, John Coode, was knighted for his work on this great scheme. Convicts laboured with the main civilian Contractor J.T. Leather and Company, and up to three thousand tons of stone a day were transported from the top of the island. Nearly six million tons of stone were used in all. The final northern breakwater was built between 1894 and 1903.

28. 'These are Imperial Works and Worthy Kings' is the inscription on the ceremonial stone laid here by H.R.H. Prince Albert on 25th July 1847. This was civil engineering work of the grandest scale, of a time when Art, Science and Engineering were considered inseparable. These monumental Portland stone arches were built to carry the railway well above the sea level 1½ miles from the land on the first two breakwaters. Between the latter was a 480 feet (146 metres) ship entrance, which during construction was spanned by a timber tressle supporting the railway 90 feet (27 metres) above the sea bed. This photograph was taken in 1905.

29. The Home Fleet of the Royal Navy in Portland Harbour (then still known as Portland Roads), in 1911. The occasion was the visit of H.M. King George V to review the fleet. The harbour was conceived in the days of sail, but by the turn of the century, and the advent of the Dreadnought battleships, the port was well adapted to the demands of coal and oil powered steamships. Projecting from the left is the 1,580 feet (480 metres) long New Admiralty Pier, built to hold and feed vast quantities of coal to the great war vessels. Coal has given way to liquid and nuclear fuels, the piers have been extended and berths depened to accommodate the largest vessels of the NATO fleets for which Portland in the 1980's is a prime working-up base.

30. A garrison is seen here emerging from the South Gate of the hilltop Verne Citadel around 1900. The uniforms were still flamboyant, but then the sobering reality of the First World War was still over a decade away. From the gate the road passed over a steel drawbridge over the 70 feet (21 metres) deep dry moat of Verne Ditch which together with the sheer cliffs on the north and east sides made the citadel virtually impregnable from land attack. Sixteen centuries earlier the Romans occupied this same site in a large earthwork encampment, but the Victorians remoulded the entire hilltop into a heavily fortified bomb-proof citadel, unkindly labelled one of Lord Palmerston's 'follies'. It was considered out of date before its completion in 1872.

31. The scale of the Verne Citadel project much of which is below ground with associated gun batteries is awe inspiring. All landward approaches were graded into defensible glacis, which involved moving hundreds of thousand of tons of earth and stone. The last soldiers left the Verne after 1945. Built with the help of convict labour, fate has turned on the Verne, for in 1949 it was converted into a civilian prison. The Victorian ramparts and masonry buildings were declared Ancient Monuments in 1974, but not before some of the finer features had been lost.

32. This is the gatehouse of Portland Prison, at the Grove, pictured some fifty years after 1848, when it was established. Convicts were first brought to Portland to labour on the construction of the breakwaters and military defences. Within a few years a large convict prison was built on this cliff edge site. Up to eleven hundred prisoners at any one time spent their days quarrying, or dressing and squaring blocks of masonry for the Government works. For many it was an alternative to transportation to the Colonies. Lofty cell blocks of whitbed stone now dominate Portland's east coast skyline. The prison was converted to a Borstal Institution in 1921. The quarters beyond the old archway were demolished in a major rebuilding scheme in 1973. The original gatehouse with its carved Royal Arms has now been incorporated as a feature in the facade of new offices.

33. When this photograph was taken at the end of the last century, Easton was a village still surrounded by farmland of small stip fields spreading out to the cliffs. A rich variety of building styles lines Easton Street, from the squat seventeenth century thatch dwellings to lofty Victorian houses. Old drawings show that ninety years previously Easton consisted mainly of low stone-gabled cottages of the type seen here on the right. This specimen was one of the few of its era to survive for a short while into the twentieth century. Fortunately enough of the charm and unusual character remained in the 1970's for Easton to be declared an 'Outstanding Conservation Area'. Tophill is characterised by very wide roads, such as this one which leads down to the focal point of Easton Square.

34. Easton Square in 1880 had hardly changed in two hundred years. A hollow in the Tophill plateau, with a tiny stream feeding a pond, where three of the island's main roads met was a natural place for early settlement. Change here over the centuries was slow and organic. Victorian buildings augmented the older cottages, to border a large square – a featureless plane created where the natural hollow had been filled with centuries of debris. What remained of the old pond was condemned as 'insanitary', and was filled in 1873 just eight years before this picture was taken. Still, Easton remained the hub of life on Tophill. Around here the main schools, chapels, shops, and in 1901 the railway station, were built. The gap between the houses (centre left) was filled a year after Queen Victoria's Diamond Jubilee by a large social club hall, named (what else?) – the Jubilee Hall.

35. Many island houses had a private well, but most did not, so with a rising population in the late nineteenth century a public water supply was desperately needed. Every Portland village had a pond or public well of sorts, and this one at Easton Square was dug by hand down into the bedrock probably before 1850. The shaft was over one hundred feet (thirty metres) deep so a hand operated pump was installed to raise the water. The closing of this well must have caused a marked drop in the pocket money earned by the Easton children who stood by to earn pennies turning the pump handle. This photograph shows the well-head and its crude canopy over the cast-iron pump mechanism in about 1903, just before it was removed and the shaft top sealed over. By now, Portland had a copious supply of fine water piped from the mainland.

36. Wednesday 18th August 1904, under brilliant sunshine the crowds gathered at Easton for the grand opening of the Gardens. This was another scheme conceived on 1896 to celebrate Victoria's Jubilee, but the problems of finding a suitable site, and of finance, delayed the work. The daily scene of stone trucks and horse-carts trundling through quiet Easton Street contrasted with the festive atmosphere that the colourful flags and people from far and wide made on that day. After Council Chairman Henry Sansom performed the opening ceremony, he hosted tea parties on his own nearby tree-lined Park Field, which incidentally he was soon to quarry away! The buildings here have changed very little in eighty years. Shops have closed, others have opened, modern traffic dominates, but the basic character of central Easton remains.

37. Looking north-east across the new Easton Gardens in 1904, the crowning centrepiece of the ornate bandstand was perfectly matched by the elegance of the local ladies. Gone was the barren wilderness of Easton Square, the contaminated old pond and the pump. Low dressed stone walls surmounted by iron railings enclosed the site and asphalted paths meandered through new lawns and spacious flower beds. Most of the £1,397 it cost to form the gardens came from surplus money invested after the rebuilding of the island's Ferrybridge. Within a few years trees – including palms – had matured to soften central Easton into an oasis by now surrounded by ever encroaching stone quarries. Band concerts were regularly enjoyed here for over sixty years. Sadly the railings and wrought iron gate were taken for war salvage, the bandstand was dismantled through want of maintenance in 1965, and much of the lawn was later asphalted over.

38. By the turn of the century an old (1845) chapel in Park Road, Easton had become quite inadequate for its purpose. A scheme for a new Wesleyan Church at Easton was inaugurated in 1902 and a pair of derelict cottages overlooking Easton Square was demolished to provide the site. Messrs. Wakeham Bros. were the builders, their other big contract here being the new lighthouse for Trinity House at Portland Bill. The new church which was completed in 1907, displays possibly the finest examples of local stonecarvers craft existing on Portland. This 1906 picture shows the timber scaffolding in place for the building of the church's twin pinnacles. Next door is the former Wesleyan day school, erected in 1878.

39. This is Weston's Pond in 1898. Until very recently this village consisted only of small groups of cottages, widely separated alongside expansive greens. The old pond was at one time well cared for, deep with rough hewn stone walls, steps and ramps. As in all ancient villages the pond was a vital feature to the residents. It was the main watering place, and was used for washing, but by the 1870's it had become dirty and unkempt. Stone from the walls had fallen into the water, the edges had become muddy and slippery and the little roadside watercourse that fed it was not enough to keep in fresh condition. The final straw was the drowning of a little boy in its waters in 1902, and understandably it was filled in soon after this. The old Prince Alfred Inn is on the right of the cottages beyond, and this was the last of that group to be demolished, in 1977.

40. Gypsy Lane at Weston is one of the most picturesque parts of Portland. This little corner, just off the main road, had two fine thatched cottages dating from about 1600. By this lane, too was the old Lugger Inn, renowned as a smuggler's haunt, and the first building on the island to have glass windows. Cottages of this period formed the core of most of the island's villages until the so-called 'slum clearance' policy earlier this century swept them all away – all that is except just one of the pair seen here and another at Wakeham which have been well preserved. Weston was basically a farming village, the main farm house being just down the road from this lane. The butcher seen here with his horse and delivery waggon in 1899 was William Morris of Fortuneswell, up from Underhill for the day.

41. Dominating the skyline in this 1980's photograph of Southwell is the remarkable little St. Andrew's Church. This was built in memorium to a tragic shipwreck in the English Channel opposite this spot in 1877. The clipper 'Avalanche' bound for New Zealand collided with the 'Forest' heading for New York. Despite heroic efforts of Portland beachmen one hundred men, women and children drowned. Within two years subscriptions from grieving relatives, friends and sympathisers were sufficient to build this beautiful and touching memorial. Beyond the trio of ladies and the baby can be seen a drystone wall, which separated the dusty road from Southwell's main pond, now long since filled. From this a little open stream flowed along Southwell's only street, through a lower pool and over the cliffs into Freshwater Bay. The road to the left leads to Barrow Hill and Sweet Hill.

42. The Bill, or Beale as it was once called, is Dorset's southernmost tip jutting far out into the English Channel. Navigation past this rocky shore has always been hazardous, the waters are amongst the most dangerous for shipping around the British Isles. Several hundred years ago, coal or wood burning beacons were lit on the nearest high ground to this point, Branscombe Hill. The first two lighthouses were erected as a working pair in 1716. This photograph is a boatman's view of the latest lighthouse erected by Trinity House in 1906 to replace two others which were built in 1869. In the centre is an obelisk, erected in 1844, as near as practicable to Bill Point as an aid to mariners, while on the left is the famous landmark known as Pulpit Rock. Two hand cranes can also be seen, for small-scale quarrying was carried on around the Bill cliffs for a while between about 1880 and 1910.

43. This little beach will be unfamiliar even to most residents of Portland. It is at Balaclava Bay, a good sheltered landing place near Portland Nor. Although some distance from the island's villages, it had naturally long been a favourite base for fishermen. This whole section of coast was acquired by the War Department in 1847, but free public access to it was maintained right up to the 1950's.To the left in this 1907 picture can be seen the cottages at one of three coastguard stations on the island at that time. The girder bridge, then only ten years old, carried the public railway which ran around the cliffs and up to Easton. This bridge passed over the Freemans Incline built to convey stone to the breakwater. The cable drum house at the top was some 400 feet (120 metres) above sea level. H.R.H. Prince Albert was drawn up this line in crimson-draped trucks after his spectacular foundation stone-laying ceremony in 1849. This area is now totally absorbed into the Naval port.

44. The seaboard of Chesil Beach looks placid enough in this 1890's view looking towards West Cliffs. Often dubbed one of the wonders of the natural world, this vast bank of shingle is constantly changing. Storms can move over four million tons of shingle overnight, transforming the seaward side in a few hours from gentle terraces to a single almost unclimbable concave slope. Generations of Portlanders have learned to respect this awesome power of the sea. The village lady standing on the crest could have been awaiting the return of her fisherman husband, to help sort the catch. The woman traditionally took all the surplus fish to Weymouth, where there was always a ready Market.

45. Portland's traditional fishing boats were the 'lerrets', like this one at Chesil Cove around 1905. These fine wide-beamed sea boats were never known to capsize. The craft were launched bow first down the shingle slope, gathering some speed before hitting the surf. In pulling, the boatmen did not keep stroke – 'each side gets on as best it can', says an 1849 report. Being sharp at both ends, beaching was done stern first, the shore-helpers heaving on a start-rope through a hole in the keel. Greased oars laid on the shingle eased the haul up. Net repairs occupied laborious hours on the beach.

46. This is the scene at Chesil Cove in January 1920, after the Greek steamer the 'Preveza' on a run between France and Rotterdam ran aground on the beach. Fishermen heard the muffled sound of the ship's siren, but before any help could be summoned the vessel loomed out of the mist to grind hard into the shingle. The crew of twenty-six was safely brought ashore, but attempts to refloat the 'Preveza' were thwarted by a fierce storm shortly after, which broke her back. In earlier times the ship would have provided good booty for Portlanders, but the 'Preveza' was legitimately broken up and sold for scrap.

47. Only twenty-four hours after the 'Preveza' foundered, the 'James Fennel', an Admiralty trawler returning from Portsmouth, came ashore at the notorious Tar Rocks, near Blacknor Point. That night of 16th January 1920 was still foggy, and the first on the scene were two local lads with their torches, Frank Morris and Cyril Patten, and fisherman Sunny Saunders, who helped the master and crew ashore, and up the precipitous cliffs to safety. The tide later carried the vessel off the jagged rocks to a watery grave, where she still lies.

48. Fog also led to this shipwreck, on the night of 27th August 1886. The master of the paddle steamer 'SS Bournemouth' clearly miscalculated his passage past Portland Bill, and his vessel hit the rocks at full speed ending up a total wreck under the cliff at Walls End Cove, on the island's west side. The air was so still that the shouts of the passengers, who had been returning to Bournemouth from a day trip to Torquay, could be heard at Weston over a mile from this spot. All one hundred and ninety-four aboard her were saved, but the neat little steamer was a total loss.

49. The shores under West Cliffs have seen countless wrecks and the loss of thousands of lives through the centuries. The steamer 'Patroclus' was one of very few vessels which survived to sail another day. She became stranded on the rocks on 13th September 1907, and the latest rocket powered life saving apparatus was used in the rescue of the crew. What cargo could not be discharged into barges and hulks was dumped into the sea, and she was towed off nine days later. To the left of the crowds lining the distant clifftop can be seen a tower. In fact this was a brick navigational landmark, the locals called it 'The Monument', and it was blown up by the Royal Engineers in 1915.

50. This dramatic picture of a ship being driven ashore in Chesil Cove represents a sight all too familiar for Portlanders in former times. This is the French vessel 'La Madeleine Tristan' which became trapped in the bay and was driven ashore under full sail on 20th September 1930. Most of her grain cargo and all her crew were saved, but she was a total loss, her hulk remaining high and dry on the beach for many years. The efficient local coastguards and the more refined life saving apparatus undoubtedly saved many lives from these later wrecks, although on this occasion the rocket line fired from the cliff top was blown inland by the gale!

51. By 21st December 1930, the storm had subsided leaving the 'La Madeleine Tristan' helplessly stranded. As often happens, the gigantic storm waves had denuded the beach in this part of the Cove, this time exposing not only the normally shingle-covered blue clay but the boilers of the 'SS Preveza', wrecked here ten years before. Successive storm waves had broken chunks off the low silty cliff in the foreground, all that stood between the ravenous sea and the cottages at the top end of Brandy Row (see photograph No. 16). Another thirty years passed before a good sound sea wall was built to protect this section of coast.

52. Portland Stone has been quarried for local use since pre-Roman times, but since the seventeenth century, when Inigo Jones used it for the Banqueting Hall at Whitehall and Sir Christopher Wren took over the island quarries for St. Paul's Cathedral, it has been world renowned. By the mid-nineteenth century most of the cliff edge quarry sites had been worked out. One part that remained untouched was a rare and attractive wooded field between Wakeham and Rufus Castle call Castle Hays Park. To the dismay of local people, who had always played and picnicked there, a quarry was opened there too, in about 1906, when this photograph was taken. Years later the land was abandoned, scarred, strewn with rubble and boulders, devoid of trees and soil. The distant promontory is Godnor Point.

53. The biggest recorded block of stone ever won from Portland quarries was this huge piece, which was reamed from the land called Inmost Hay in July 1906. Good quarrying requires considerable skill. Account must be taken of the natural run of joints and the different characteristics of each bed. A team of twenty-four brawny tanned men, each driving four wedges, was required to separate this block from its bed. The stone would have been further split and roughly shaped before being lifted out by a steam powered crane.

54. 'The Quarries Express'! Before any good stone could be obtained a vast quantity of rubble overburden had to be removed. Traditionally this was either tipped over the cliffs or built up into huge banks called 'beaches'. A network of narrow guage railway lines was laid out during the last century to take the rubble from the quarries to the tips. Most trucks were horsedrawn, but one innovation was this little engine, built in 1865 for a tramway in North Wales, which was later brought to Portland and ran for many years between quarries in the Weston area and West Cliff.

55. An early traction engine is seen hauling a stone waggon past the Drill Hall at Easton Lane. The introduction in Portland of modern steam technology in the 1880's brought a welcome relief to the use of horses for drawing stone, which had earlier been described as most cruel, owing to the steepness of the hills and the rough roads. The truck here was of a truly ancient design, having a strong wooden carriage, solid wheels and no brakes. Although the Drill Hall was built for the serious business of training local Volunteer Defence Units, its designer of 1868 clearly had great fun with his castellated embellishments, on what is one of Portland's most unusual buildings.

56. By the 1920's, when this picture was taken at Straits, Easton, traction engines were a familiar part of the island scene. Their enormous weight on iron wheels caused much damage to local roads. In the late 1920's a new Road Traffic Act banning most hard-wheeled vehicles ended the reign of these fascinating monsters almost overnight. The houses in this road date from the eighteenth century, but Victorian additions gave richness and variety to the street. The view in the 1980's is altered only by colourwashed walls, and of course modern transport.

57. On a visit to Portland in 1804, the Reverend J. Skinner of Bath remarked on the cruel use of horses for the drawing of stone: 'All this labour might be obviated by the simple construction of a railroad'. In October 1826 several stone merchants opened a railway to convey stone from Priory at the top of the hill down to the north shore at Castletown. Designed by civil engineer James Brown, this project was a masterpiece of simplicity and efficiency. This photograph shows the main loading point at Priory just before 1900. The stone was brought to here on horse or engine drawn waggons, loaded onto flat bed trucks and pulled by horses around the slopes of Verne Hill. The gradient was almost imperceptable, so great weights were pulled with little effort. This hand crane, which could lift up to ten tons, had a stump anchored well into the ground. It was later replaced by a sheerleg type, used until the line closed in 1939.

58. The Merchant's Railway, glimpsed here on the lower right, crosses the steep Old Hill path to pass the island's eighteenth century Rectory. High on the hill above Fortuneswell commanding the distant sweep of Chesil Bank, no ecclesiastical residence could have enjoyed a finer view. The late nineteenth century Belle Vue Terrace, lower left, the steepest row of houses on the island, climbs roof over roof to terminate in the Traveller's Rest Public House. After skirting around the head of Tilley Coombe the rail track continues around the side of Verne Hill opposite, marked by a parapet of heavy stone boulders.

59. To traverse the final steep hillside from Verne Common to Castletown, an inclined plane arrangement was devised on the Merchants Railway. The horses were unhitched at the top of the slope, and chains – later steel ropes – were attached to the laden trucks. The chain was passed around a large drum brake mechanism, and down over rollers between the rails to a string of empty trucks far below, as can be seen here (centre) in Edwardian days. Gravity was thus the only force employed to move the stone over this last section. This was the oldest railway in Dorset, and it was very profitable for the stone merchants' company. The stone trade came to a virtual standstill with the onset of the Second World War, and the Merchants Railway fell victim to this in 1939. The railway bed is preserved as a footpath, but the last rails and the footbridge were removed in the 1960's.

60. This is the Stone Pier at Castletown in about 1898. Many piers have been built around the Portland shores. Some were soon destroyed by raging seas, others were maintained for centuries, but this is one of only two to survive into the twentieth century. Replacing the original timber pier, it was built on Crown foreshore at the end of the line from the Merchants Incline. Hundreds of thousands of tons of Portland stone were taken from here to provide the fabric for some of London's most famous streets and buildings. The unusual little sail boats seen here are on what remained of the long Castletown Beach, after most of the northern shoreline was built on for the naval base.

61. The arrival of motor transport opened up new horizons for Portland families in the 1920's. Until then for many islanders a trip to the mainland was a major excursion. Enterprising local drivers acquired open 'chara-bancs' and started frequent trips to far-flung outposts of the West Country and to the Capital. Well dressed passengers were photographed setting off – it was always an event worth recording (while hats were still in place!) This trip was from Victoria Square, also the scene of regular hoards of sailors, train passengers and soldiers from the Verne arriving and departing. Behind is a little tea-room in the centre of Victoria Buildings, a neat terrace dating from the 1880's.

62. Long before stone and the navy became the island's staple industries, farming and fishing were the main living. The special breed of Portland sheep was renowned. John Hutchins wrote in 1774 that Portland mutton was esteemed 'some of the best in England'. Roaming freely on the common lands over Verne Hill and sure-footedly around the cliffs and weares of the island, the flocks were shepherded down to the Mere near Chiswell for washing prior to shearing. More than sixty years after this photograph was taken, a small flock of true Portland sheep was successfully re-introduced onto the island. One legacy of the sheep farming industry is in some island place names, like 'Sheep Croft' and 'Shepherds Dinner'.

63. The Mere, pictured here in 1906, was a tidal inlet from Portland Roads, its opening being between the sand and shingle arms of Conygar Bank. Most of its area dried out at normal low tide leaving a central creek-like channel called the 'Gut'. This was one of the last recorded sheep washings, for not only had quarrying destroyed most grazing areas without hope of restoration, but the Admiralty was then already starting to fill in the Mere to gain valuable flat land. This took place in the face of strong protests about the effect this filling would have on the flooding of nearby Chiswell. This spot is now in the centre of the nation's largest naval helicopter station.

64. While most streets had their small general shops, much trading on Portland was done by roundsmen. Here is the author's great-grandfather delivering meat from his Fortuneswell shop to the villagers of Chiswell in about 1896. Business was hard and hours were long, all for little reward. Meat and dairy products were kept 'fresh' with huge ice blocks brought from Weymouth. Butcher William Morris, also concocted a 'cure-all' remedy for a wide range of ailments, which proved a useful sideline. The houses here were between Big and Little Opes – two of the lanes leading up to the beach. Despite frequent sea floodings, these solid walled houses remained quite sound until demolished for a vague redevelopment scheme between 1930 and 1970. This now derelict part of the ancient fishing village is now awaiting a careful injection of new life.

65. For many generations the old George Inn at Reforne was the venue for the meetings and dinners of the Local Court Leet. Now almost unique in England, this body has guarded the rights and privileges of the Portland commoners without a break for a thousand years. Twenty-four jurymen selected from landowning 'tenants of the Royal Manor', a foreman, a reeve and Chief Constable, together with the Crown Bailiff, the court makes the rules and preserves the customs regulating Portland's extensive common lands. The King or Queen is the lord of the manor, but even the Crown must heed the wishes of the island's commoners as expressed through the Court Leet. Among the members of this 1900 Court were farmers, a barber, a mason, quarrymen, a grocer, a draper and a grave-digger. The reeve staff (held centre) was the device for recording payments of dues from the different areas of the island. The charming George Inn, formerly the Parish Clerk's house, dates from the early 1600's, but was enlarged in the eighteenth and nineteenth centuries.

66. Portland had a railway link to the mainland for exactly one hundred years, 1865 to 1965. During that time it played a big part in ending the historic isolation of the island people. The scheme for a branch line to the peninsula was put to a meeting at the Royal Hotel, Weymouth on 7th October 1861, and work on the four and a half mile link started a year later. A 27 span timber viaduct was built across the water at Small Mouth and the single track was laid alongside the road on the narrow causeway, to terminate at Victoria Square. The train seen here is heading for Weymouth on the embankment which was just high enough to be clear of spring tides. The notorious sea flooding of the low lying area behind the Portland end of Chesil Beach severely damaged the line a number of times. However, as the embankment near Portland Station had dammed up the free passage of floodwater to the harbour, perhaps this was some natural justice!

67. Portland's first railway station stands here in 1905 in what appears to be a ploughed field. Actually the ruts and puddles were in Victoria Square, belying the elegance of the buildings at the island's entrance. The Square bustled with sailors on shore leave and visitors arriving or awaiting transport to Weymouth. The station, built in 1864, was exquisitely proportioned with stone-mullioned windows, ornamental barge-boards and twin gables. The Admiralty had laid a working track around the coast to Castletown in 1876 and in 1900 a line climbing the East Weares and cliffs to the top of the island was completed. This original terminus was awkwardly placed for that extension so a new timber passenger station was built nearby in 1904, on a tight curve, while this 1865 building was converted to a goods depot. It was demolished in 1969, just four years after the last train left Portland.

68. The railway from Chesil Beach to Easton took over fourteen years to complete, the gradient being up to nearly three per cent, but the result was one of the most scenic lines on the British coast. However, it was a costly operation, much of the ascent being formed on notoriously unstable Kimmeridge clay. Slips were frequent, one in 1907 dropping the line by 45 feet (14 metres) on the curve under Grove Cliff. An automatic wire-trippled signalling device warned approaching trains of such landslips, so tragedies were averted. From the cliffs north of here Sir Christopher Wren took the bulk of the stone for St. Paul's Cathedral (1675 to 1717). Ancient stone circles, monoliths, and what was described as a Druid's slab existed in this area before the building of the old prison, supporting Portland folk-lore that this was the centre of the pagan worship on the island.

69. At this point the cliff-hugging line plunges abruptly between rock, on its way to the centre of Tophill. This sheer cutting, blasted into Yelland Cliff near Long Tout, turned passengers' heads from the stunning panorama across the sea to Dorset's Purbeck coast. Below lies quiet Church Ope Cove. The passenger service to Portland ended in 1952. Goods traffic continued for another thirteen years, but the line closed for ever in 1965 with a series of special train runs for enthusiasts. With the track removed and the line sold off, the opportunity for the bed to be retained for recreational use was lost, and the impressive rock cutting was filled with stone-rubble in 1975.

70. We have now arrived at Easton Station, soon after its opening to passengers in 1902. The first station master's pride shows clearly in the neat flower beds laid out under the newly-painted fence. His successor extended this by housing a unique collection of fossils in a waiting room. Being in a cutting, waiting passengers, like this Edwardian lady with her parasol, could sit on the platform sheltered from the island's sea breezes. Who, then, could have imagined that within a lifetime this railway, its buildings, bridges and noisy sidings – such an essential part of everyday life, could be declared 'unnecessary' and would vanish almost without trace. An elderly persons' home now occupies the site which was carved out of the close called Lady Mead for Easton Station.

71. *...there lies on the east side of the Island a tiny green wooded dell, which for charm and picturesqueness can hardly be surpassed. This is the Cove of Church Ope. The glen is narrow and full of shade, a most gentle hollow in the cliffs opening to the see...,* the words of traveller Sir Frederick Treves. The cove itself is reached either by a flight of one hundred and twenty-five steps, made by the Council in 1906, or by scrambling down rough pathways. The surrounding Weares present a rich botanical garden of stunted species, only fully appreciated at close quarters. The Cove was for centuries the scene of stone-shipping from now long lost piers, of fishing, of illicit landings and smuggling. When the photograph was taken around the 1920's, full time fishing from this beach had already declined. Fishermen's huts are now used for recreation.

72. The serious business of fishing, and the shipping of stone from Church Ope Cove has given way in the twentieth century to recreation. For Portlanders today, this is a favourite spot for swimming and peaceful relaxation. An amazing sight before the First War was the visit of a paddle steamer from Weymouth, which nosed onto the pebbles, landing its passengers for a stroll, and a fund raising tea in the grounds of Pennsylvania Castle on the plateau above. This was a calm sunny July day in 1911. The promontary behind is Church Point.

73. The year is around 1890 and cattle graze passively below Rufus Castle. This enigmatic pile is shrouded in mystery. Perched on a commanding rock pinnacle high above Church Ope, the castle was built for the monarch some time before the fifteenth century as a fortress against invaders from the sea. For its first centuries it was the symbol of the King's holding of the Royal Manor of Portland. What remains is only part of a larger fortress extending inland into the field called Castle Hays. In 1799, King George III gave all this land to governor John Penn. The original crumbling Norman style arch was then rebuilt with a mock Tudor one, and Penn added a stone bridge across the chasm from Castle Hays. The Castle is now a protected Ancient Monument, but the land behind it has been quarried, so destroying any clues as to the extent of the original fortress.

74. This 1903 view shows the ruin of Portland's first church, in its idyllic setting. At the foot of a narrow wooded glen, overlooked by the later Rufus Castle and the later still Pennsylvania Castle, twelfth century St. Andrews Church rests on a natural shelf overlooking Church Ope Cove. It was precarious too, as a survey of 1625 recorded, *...for saftie of it they have been forced to wall the Church Yarde Banks almost of an incredible height.* Replaced by the fine St. Georges Church at Reforne in 1766, this old building soon became what the Victorians loved as a 'romantic ruin' with mysterious steps and ivy-clad tumbled arches. What now remains of this ancient monument has now been superbly restored by local efforts.

75. Captain John Penn accompanied his friend King George III on one of his many visits to the Royal Manor of Portland. The beauty of the knapps, cliffs and wooded dell overlooking Church Ope Cove was well-known to His Majesty who duly offered the land to John Penn. The offer was readily accepted and in 1799 Squire Penn engaged famous architect James Wyatt to design the fine residence, Pennsylvania Castle, seen here one hundred years later. Little obstacles like a group of cottages and the main road to Southwell were soon removed from the site and the estate was walled in. Having lost part of their ancient village of Wakeham, the islanders at least made sure they did not lose one inch of the adjoining common land over which they had historic rights. Penn took an active part in Island life and died in 1834. His Gothic mansion was made an hotel in the 1950's.

76. These faces of a previous generation of Portlanders smile at us across time. The delightfully sheltered setting, in the grounds of Underhill's Brackenbury Church, rejoiced in the name of 'Under Hole'! Most of the fashion outfits would have been made at home or by the skilled island milliners and dressmakers. These were not high society ladies, but ordinary folk of Fortuneswell, connected with businesses, fishing and stone dressed up for a special occasion. It is a pity that colour photography had not then arrived! Not many years before, finest silks were part of the island smugglers' trade.